MIGHTY MINIBEASTS

Flies

Debbie and Brendan Gallagher

Marshall Cavendish
Benchmark
New York

This edition first published in 2012 in the United States of America by Marshall Cavendish Benchmark
An imprint of Marshall Cavendish Corporation

Website: www.marshallcavendish.us

Other Marshall Cavendish Offices:
Marshall Cavendish Ltd. 5th Floor, 32-38 Saffron Hill, London EC1N 8 FH, UK • Marshall Cavendish International (Asia) Private Limited, 1 New Industrial Road, Singapore 536196 • Marshall Cavendish International (Thailand) Co Ltd. 253 Asoke, 12th Flr, Sukhumvit 21 Road, Klongtoey Nua, Wattana, Bangkok 10110, Thailand • Marshall Cavendish (Malaysia) Sdn Bhd, Times Subang, Lot 46, Subang Hi-Tech Industrial Park, Batu Tiga, 40000 Shah Alam, Selangor Darul Ehsan, Malaysia

Library of Congress Cataloging-in-Publication Data

Gallagher, Debbie, 1969–
Flies / Debbie Gallagher.
p. cm. — (Mighty minibeasts)
Includes index.
Summary: "Discusses the features, habitat, food, life cycle, living habits, and unique behaviors of flies"—Provided by publisher.
ISBN 978-1-60870-545-0
1. Flies—Juvenile literature. I. Title.
QL533.2 .G35 2012
595.77—dc22

2010037194

First published in 2011 by
MACMILLAN EDUCATION AUSTRALIA PTY LTD
15–19 Claremont Street, South Yarra 3141

Visit our website at www.macmillan.com.au or go directly to www.macmillanlibrary.com.au

Associated companies and representatives throughout the world.

Publisher: Carmel Heron
Commissioning Editor: Niki Horin
Managing Editor: Vanessa Lanaway
Editor: Tim Clarke
Proofreader: Gill Owens
Designer: Kerri Wilson (cover and text)
Page layout: Domenic Lauricella
Photo research: Legendimages
Illustrator: Gaston Vanzet
Production Controller: Vanessa Johnson

Printed in China

Acknowledgments
The authors and the publisher are grateful to the following for permission to reproduce copyright material:

Front cover photograph: A robberfly © Dreamstime.com/Orionmystery.

Photographs courtesy of: ANTPhoto.com.au/Jurgen Otto, **11** (bottom right), /Otto Rogge, **23**; Dreamstime.com/Ariel Bravy, **18**, /Djay712, **20**, /Frebeat, **21** (top), /Hakoar, **12**, /Hudakore, **6**, /Iceshaman, **28**, /Mirceax, **21** (bottom), /Orionmystery, **1**, **11** (top right), /Horia Vlad Bogdan, **9**; Entomart, **7**, **11** (top left); iStockphoto/herrumbroso, **21** (center below); Richard E. Lee, Jr, **10** (bottom); National Geographic Stock/Joel Sartore, **25**; Photolibrary/Mark Chappell, **10** (top), /Fabio Colombini Medeiros, **14** (top), /Tristan Da Cunha, **19**, /Geoff Higgins, **17**, /John Mitchell, **15** (top), /Darlyne A Murawski, **15** (bottom), /RNagel, **22**, /Jerry Pavia, **29**, /Photo Researchers, **13**, /SPL, **14** (bottom), /SPL/Dr Keith Wheeler, **8** (bottom), /Scott W Smith, **8** (top), /Stuart Wilson, **11** (bottom left); Pixmac/Keith Frith, **30**; Shutterstock/errni, **5**, /Cathy Keifer, **24**, /Daleen Loest, **21** (center above), **27**, /Dr Morley Read, **3**, **4**, **16**.

1 3 5 6 4 2

Contents

When a word is printed in **bold**, you can look up its meaning in the Glossary on page 31.

Mighty Minibeasts

Minibeasts are small animals, such as flies and spiders. Although they are small, minibeasts are a mighty collection of animals. They belong to three animal groups: arthropods, molluscs, or annelids.

	Animal Group		
	Arthropods	**Molluscs**	**Annelids**
Main Feature	Arthropods have an outer skeleton and a body that is divided into sections.	Most molluscs have a soft body that is not divided into sections.	Annelids have a soft body made up of many sections.
Examples of Minibeasts	Insects, such as ants, beetles, cockroaches, and wasps **Arachnids**, such as spiders and scorpions Centipedes and millipedes	Snails and slugs	Earthworms Leeches

More than three-quarters of all animals are minibeasts!

Flies

Flies are minibeasts. They belong to the arthropod group of animals. This means they have an outer skeleton and a body divided into sections. Flies are a type of insect.

Flies are closely related to mayflies and dragonflies.

What Do Flies Look Like?

Flies have a body that is divided into three main parts. These parts are the head, the **thorax**, and the **abdomen**. They have two wings and six legs.

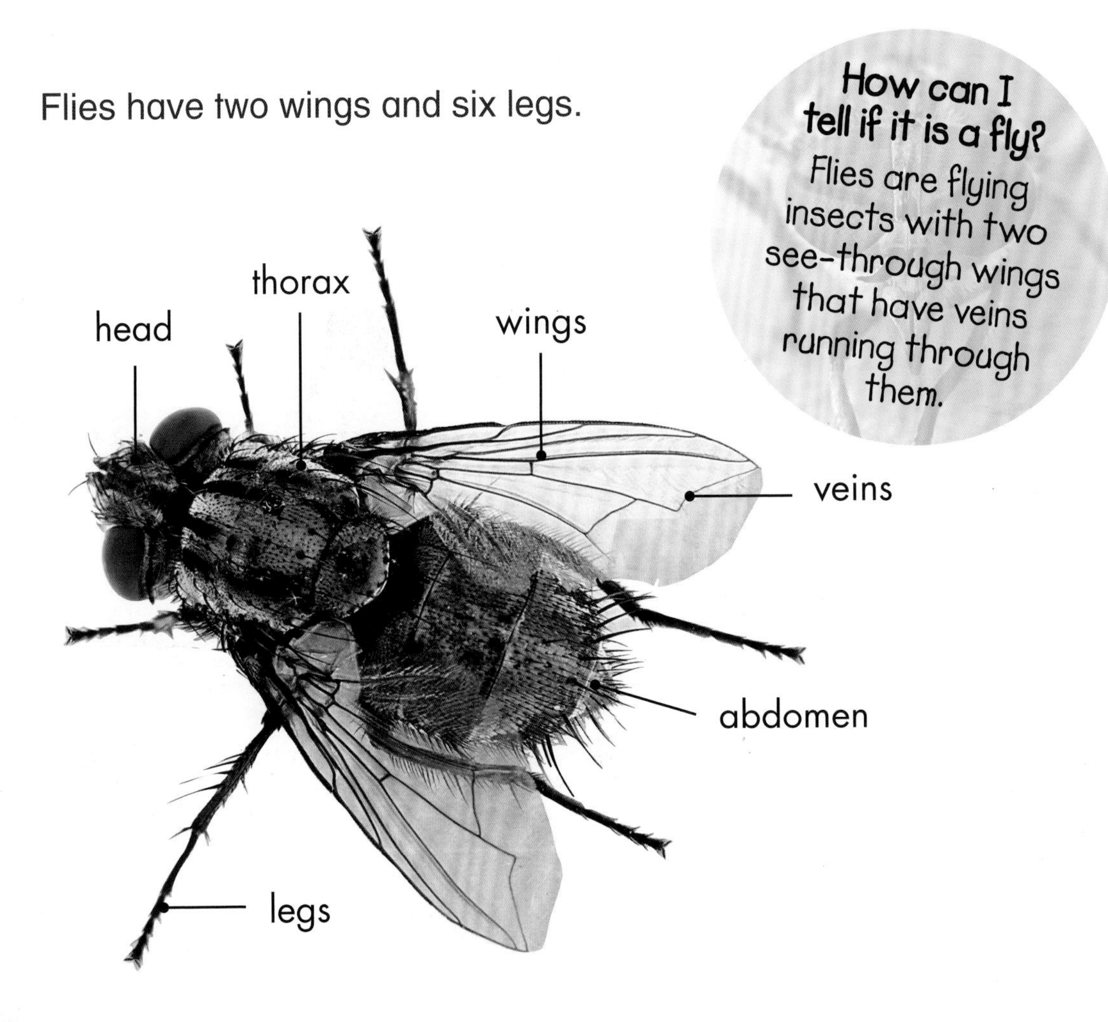

Flies have two wings and six legs.

Flies have two special eyes called compound eyes. Compound eyes are made up of lots of tiny eyes. Flies also have **antennae** on their head.

Flies use their special features to sense the world around them.

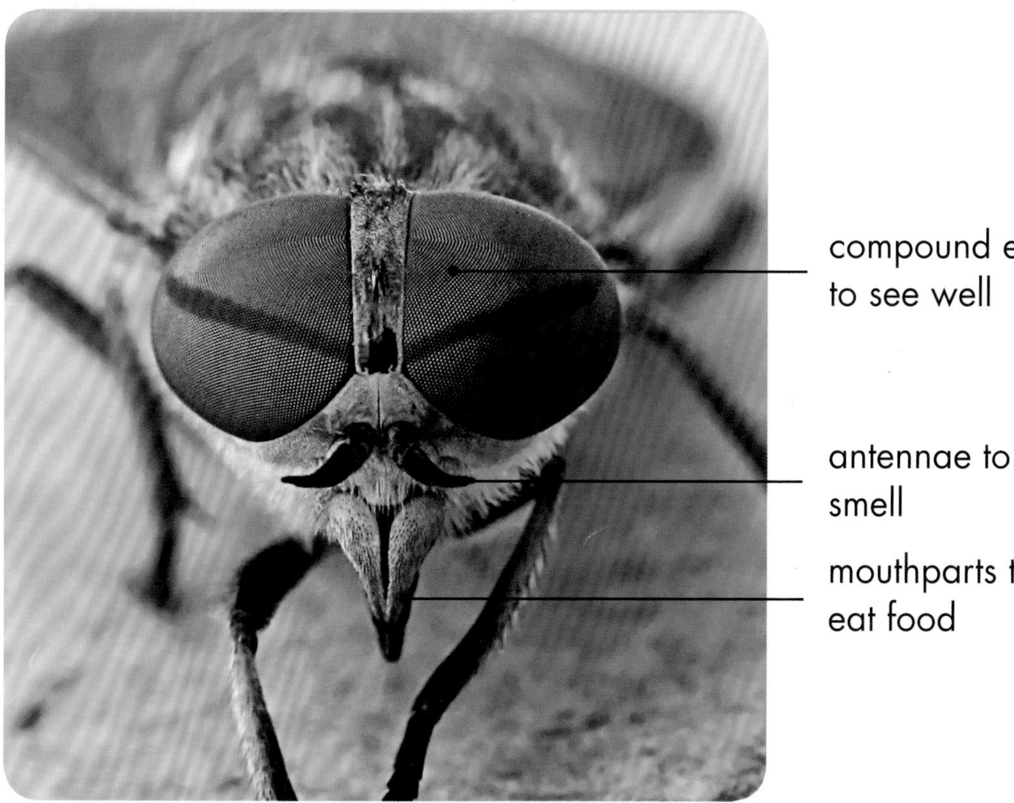

Different Types of Flies

There are more than 150,000 different **species** of flies. They can be as small as 1/24 inch (1 millimeter) long to as large as 2½ inches (6.5 centimeters) long.

Crane flies are one of the largest species of fly.

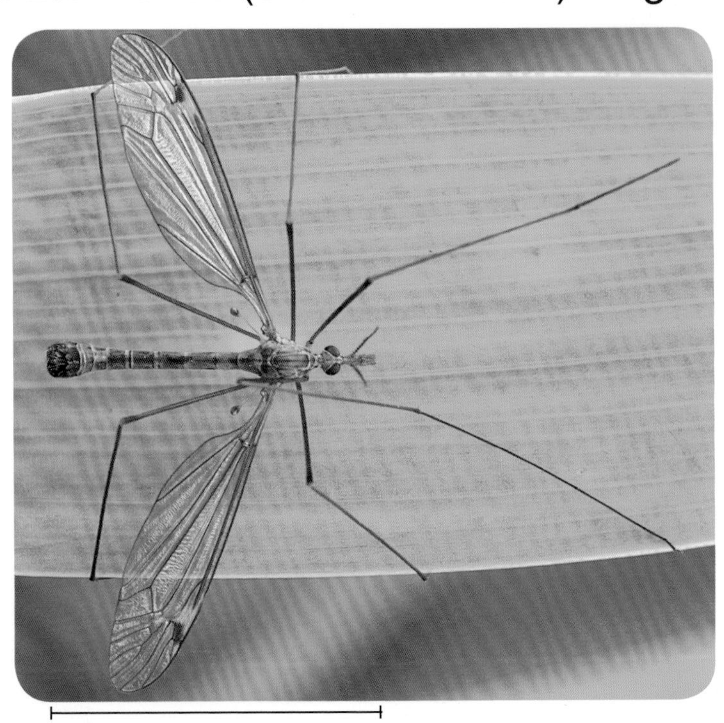

2½ inches (6.5 centimeters)

1/24 inch (1 millimeter)

Midges are sometimes called "no-see-ums" because they are so small and hard to see.

Many types of insect have the word *fly* in their name, such as butterfly and firefly. However, these minibeasts are not flies because they have more than one pair of wings.

Dragonflies have four wings, so they are not a type of fly.

Where in the World Are Flies Found?

Flies can be found on all continents, including parts of Antarctica. They can also be found on most islands.

The Antarctic midge is one of just a few animals that can live in Antarctica. Even though it is only 1/12 inch (2 millimeters) long, it is Antarctica's largest land animal!

Habitats of Flies

Flies live in all types of **habitats**. They live in forests, up mountains, on beaches, and in many deserts. Some species of fly young can even live in boiling water!

Hoverflies need flowers in their habitat to survive.

Some species of flies live in human habitats such as farms and towns. These species include some fruit flies, houseflies, bluebottles, and mosquitoes.

Fruit flies are attracted to fruit in people's homes.

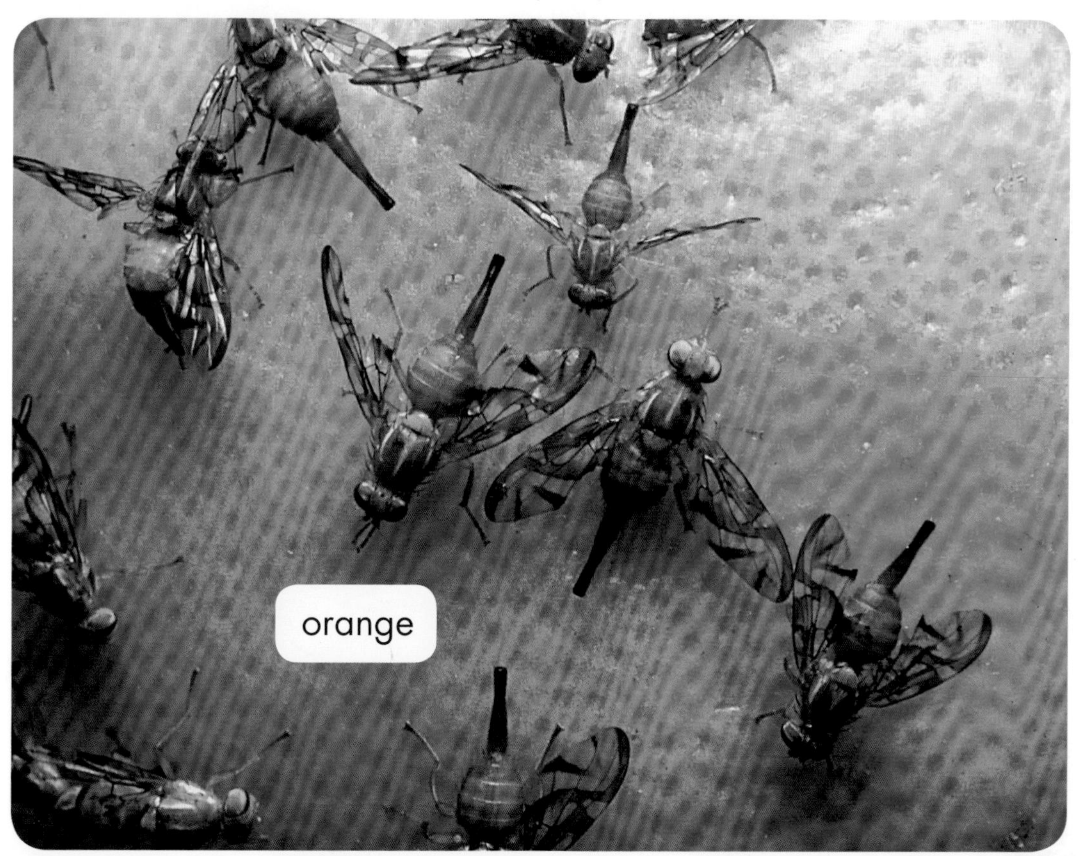

Life Cycles of Flies

A life cycle diagram shows the stages of a fly's life, from newborn to adult.

1. A male and a female fly **mate**. The female lays eggs in a place where the young will have food to eat.

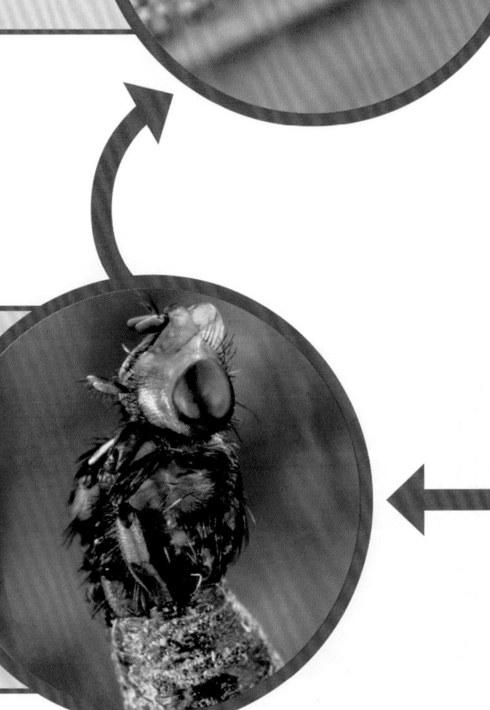

4. The pupa stage can last from a few hours to a few weeks. When it is ready, each fly emerges fully grown from its cocoon.

Most flies live for only a few days, while some live for a few months. During this time they must mate and lay eggs that will hatch into new flies.

2. **Larvae** (say *lar-vee*) hatch from the eggs and eat until they have grown to full size. The larvae change their skin several times as they grow. This is called molting.

3. When the larvae reach full size, they form a hard casing called a cocoon around themselves. At this stage they are called **pupae** (say *pyoo-pee*).

How Do Flies Live?

Nearly all species of flies live on their own. They spend their lives flying around, looking for food. When they find food, they taste it using the hairs on their feet.

Flies use their feet to taste any food they find.

Some flies swarm together. They usually do this around sunset. Most swarms are made up of male flies trying to attract female flies.

Swarms of flies can contain hundreds of flies.

Fly Homes

Flies do not make homes to live in. When they need to rest, they take shelter. Flies take shelter on walls and fences, under leaves, or in trees.

Flies can use their sticky feet to hang upside down when they need to rest.

Flies live near the types of food they like to eat. Female flies lay their eggs near or on food. Fly young can eat this food when they hatch.

Flies lay their eggs on food such as meat, which young flies can eat when they hatch.

Fly Food

Flies cannot chew, so their food must be in liquid form. They use a **proboscis** to suck up liquid food. Many flies only feed on **nectar** and **pollen**.

This bee fly is using its proboscis to drink nectar from a flower.

Flies spit a special juice onto solid food. This juice turns the food into a liquid. The fly then sucks up the liquid food.

How Do Flies Fly So Well?

Flies can fly very well. This is because they beat their wings very quickly using strong muscles.

Some midges can beat their wings one thousand times per second.

Flies can hover in the air, which means they can stay flying in the same position. They can also turn around while hovering. Flies can even fly backward and upside down!

This hoverfly is able to hover by beating its wings very quickly.

Threats to the Survival of Flies

Flies are threatened by other animals. Many different **predators** feed on flies, such as birds, spiders, and toads. Many fly predators will also eat fly eggs, larvae, and pupae.

Jumping spiders feed on fruit flies.

The survival of some species of flies is threatened by humans. When people build farms and cities, fly habitats may be lost. Some fly species that have lost their habitats are now **extinct**.

The Delhi Sands flower-loving fly is nearly extinct due to habitat loss in the United States.

Flies and the Environment

Flies are an important part of the **environment** they live in. Flies feed on other animals and on plants, and many animals feed on them. This is shown in a food web.

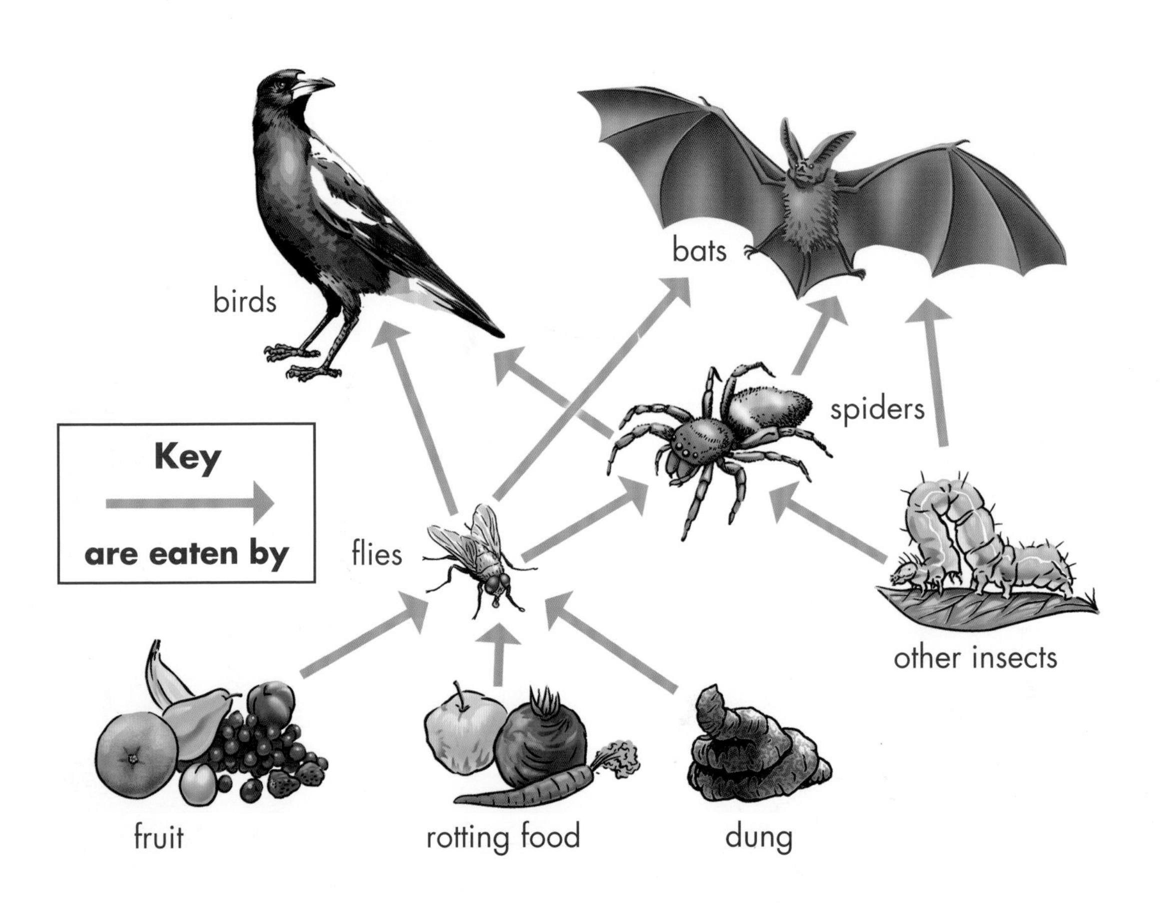

This food web shows what flies eat and what eats them.

Flies help to break down animal droppings, called dung, and rotting foods in their environment. They change this waste into soil. However, flies that eat dung and rotting foods can spread diseases.

Flies help to break down waste by feeding on animal dung.

Flies and Pollination

Some species of fly help to **pollinate** flowers. Flies visit flowers to drink their nectar. Pollen sticks to their body and is carried to other flowers. This helps create new plants.

This fly is picking up pollen on its body while drinking the flower's nectar.

Chocolate is made using the seeds of the cacao tree. The cacao tree can only be pollinated by one species of fly. Without this fly there would be no chocolate.

Flies help cacao trees to make new plants.

Tips for Watching Flies

These tips will help you to watch flies:

- Choose a warm, sunny day when flies are more likely to be out in the open.
- Look for flies where there are flowers, such as in a garden or a park.
- Put out some old food and wait for the flies to come.
- Flies are good at seeing movement, so move slowly so you do not disturb them.

Look but do not touch!
Watch flies without touching them to see where they go and what they do.

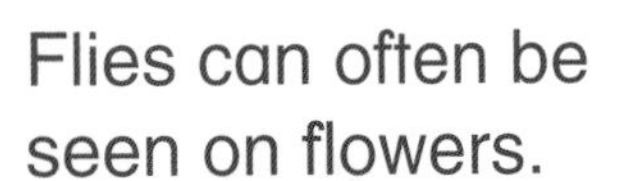

Flies can often be seen on flowers.

Glossary

abdomen The end section of an insect's body.

antennae Organs found on the heads of insects, used for sensing things.

arachnids Eight-legged animals, such as spiders, that are part of the arthropod group.

environment The air, water, and land that surround us.

extinct No longer alive on the planet.

habitats Areas in which animals are naturally found.

larvae The young of an insect.

mate Join together to produce young.

nectar A sweet liquid made by flowers.

pollen Yellow powder found on flowers.

pollinate To share pollen between plants, which helps create new plants.

predators Animals that hunt other animals for food.

proboscis A tube used for sucking up food.

pupae What insect larvae turn into before becoming adults.

species Groups of animals or plants that have similar features.

thorax The part of the body between the head and abdomen.

Index